THE STORY OF THE
BALTIMORE RAVENS

NFL TODAY

THE STORY OF THE BALTIMORE RAVENS

AARON FRISCH

CREATIVE EDUCATION

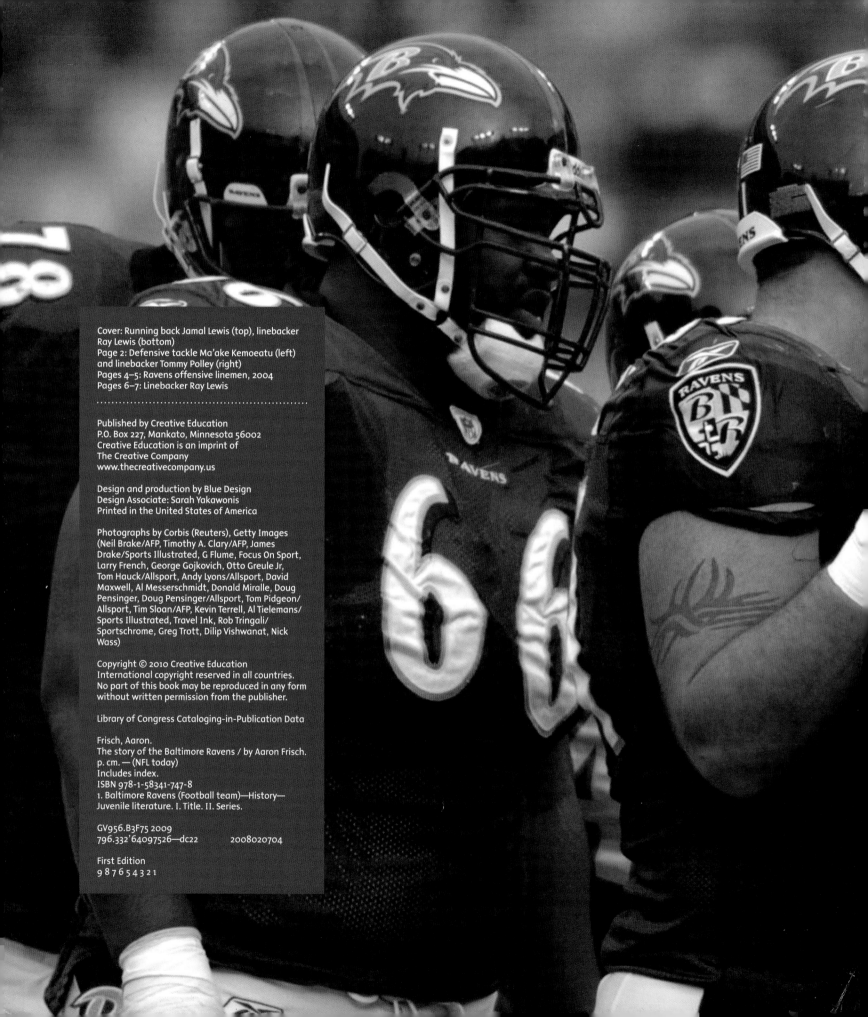

Cover: Running back Jamal Lewis (top), linebacker
Ray Lewis (bottom)
Page 2: Defensive tackle Ma'ake Kemoeatu (left)
and linebacker Tommy Polley (right)
Pages 4–5: Ravens offensive linemen, 2004
Pages 6–7: Linebacker Ray Lewis

....

Published by Creative Education
P.O. Box 227, Mankato, Minnesota 56002
Creative Education is an imprint of
The Creative Company
www.thecreativecompany.us

Design and production by Blue Design
Design Associate: Sarah Yakawonis
Printed in the United States of America

Photographs by Corbis (Reuters), Getty Images
(Neil Brake/AFP, Timothy A. Clary/AFP, James
Drake/Sports Illustrated, G Flume, Focus On Sport,
Larry French, George Gojkovich, Otto Greule Jr,
Tom Hauck/Allsport, Andy Lyons/Allsport, David
Maxwell, Al Messerschmidt, Donald Miralle, Doug
Pensinger, Doug Pensinger/Allsport, Tom Pidgeon/
Allsport, Tim Sloan/AFP, Kevin Terrell, Al Tielemans/
Sports Illustrated, Travel Ink, Rob Tringali/
Sportschrome, Greg Trott, Dilip Vishwanat, Nick
Wass)

Library of Congress Cataloging-in-Publication Data

Frisch, Aaron.
The story of the Baltimore Ravens / by Aaron Frisch.
p. cm. — (NFL today)
Includes index.
ISBN 978-1-58341-747-8
1. Baltimore Ravens (Football team)—History—
Juvenile literature. I. Title. II. Series.

GV956.B3F75 2009
796.332'64097526—dc22   2008020704

First Edition
9 8 7 6 5 4 3 2 1

CONTENTS

ON THE SIDELINES

MEET THE RAVENS

COLTS OUT, RAVENS IN

X --

Baltimore, Maryland, was founded on Chesapeake Bay in 1729 as a seaport for shipping tobacco and grain. In 1814, U.S. soldiers bravely defended Baltimore's Fort McHenry against a fierce British naval barrage—a battle that inspired Francis Scott Key to write the poem that later became "The Star-Spangled Banner," America's national anthem. Later, Baltimore produced baseball legend Babe Ruth and also became known for its great horse-racing tradition and its world-famous Johns Hopkins Hospital.

Another part of Baltimore's rich history involves professional football. From 1953 until 1983, the city's sports fans cheered for the Baltimore Colts of the National Football League (NFL). But despite winning three NFL championships and enjoying great fan support during most of their existence, the Colts moved to Indianapolis in 1984 after team owner Robert Irsay expressed unhappiness with Baltimore's Memorial Stadium. Baltimore lost its team but never gave up on its dream of having another. The city maintained Memorial Stadium, and 11 years later, it received welcome news. In 1995, the Cleveland Browns announced that they would relocate and become the Baltimore Ravens.

The Browns had been a member of the NFL since 1950, but by the early 1990s, team owner Art Modell had decided

X Baltimore has a long history as a key American seaport; besides its role in shipping food and other vital products, the city has built and launched many of America's warships.

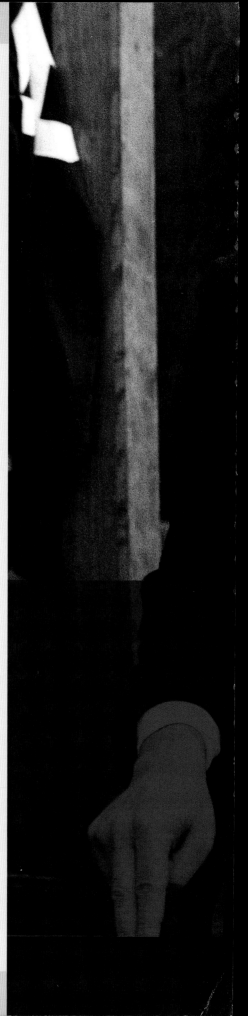

his team could no longer compete financially playing in aging Cleveland Municipal Stadium. In 1996, after he and the city failed to reach a financing agreement to build a new home for the Browns, Modell moved his team to Baltimore, where a new stadium would be built. In moving to Baltimore, Modell agreed to let Cleveland keep the Browns name, colors, and records. "The Browns name, and everything that goes with it, will stay in Cleveland," Modell said.

To help determine a new team name, a Baltimore newspaper conducted a survey to gather suggestions. "Americans" and "Marauders" were popular choices, but in the end, the new team was named the Ravens. A raven is a large black bird of great intelligence that often appears purple in the sunlight. One of Baltimore's most famous citizens, author Edgar Allan Poe, portrayed a talking raven as the title character in his classic poem "The Raven."

The Browns-turned-Ravens came to Baltimore with their full player roster intact, but Modell decided to replace Browns coach Bill Belichick. He selected a familiar face to fill the position: Ted Marchibroda, who had coached the old Colts team from 1975 to 1979. Marchibroda, an enthusiastic leader, was charged with turning around a team that had finished just 5–11 in its final season in Cleveland. The veteran coach

ART MODELL

TEAM OWNER
RAVENS SEASONS: 1996-2004

Art Modell was a rarity, one of the last NFL owners to own a team as his primary profession rather than as a hobby or side interest. Born in 1925, Modell became wealthy through television production and advertising. He bought the Cleveland Browns franchise in 1961 (for $4 million) and helped the NFL become a major television attraction. His Browns won the NFL championship in 1964 and remained a beloved—if not always successful—institution in Cleveland in the decades that followed. But in 1996, Modell moved the franchise to Baltimore after he and Cleveland could not agree to terms on financing a new stadium. Cleveland fans vilified him for it, and Modell himself called it "an agonizing moment," but he claimed his only options were to either move the team or go bankrupt. Modell found a warm reception in Baltimore and became a local hero of sorts after the Ravens won Super Bowl XXXV in January 2001. Although many people believe Modell deserves a place in the Pro Football Hall of Fame, numerous voting sportswriters—upset by Modell's franchise relocation—have declined to cast ballots for his induction.

STARS, STALLIONS, AND BOMBERS

From 1953 to 1983, Baltimore was a thriving football town, the proud home of the three-time NFL champion Baltimore Colts. When the Colts moved to Indianapolis in 1983, fans were crushed. In the decade that followed, Baltimore was represented by two football teams in minor pro leagues—the Stars of the United States Football League (USFL) and the Stallions of the Canadian Football League (CFL), both of which won league championships—but it wasn't the same. In 1989, the NFL announced that it would be expanding by two franchises for the 1995 season. Officials in Baltimore launched an effort to land one of the franchises, going so far as to determine a team name—the Bombers—and develop a logo, which featured a military aircraft over a gold sunburst that resembled an explosion. Baltimore was one of five cities narrowed down as finalists, but in the end, the expansion franchises went to Charlotte, North Carolina, and Jacksonville, Florida, instead. When Baltimore finally got its team with the 1996 relocation of the Cleveland Browns, the shield-like logo of the Bombers was incorporated into the design of the original Ravens logo.

knew he could count on quarterback Vinny Testaverde to provide steady offensive leadership, and hard-hitting safety Stevon Moore was an anchor around which the defense could be built. Still, Marchibroda knew the Ravens would need an infusion of young talent if they were to rise in the American Football Conference (AFC) Central Division, which was frequently dominated by the Pittsburgh Steelers.

In the 1996 NFL Draft, the Ravens used their two top picks to acquire giant offensive tackle Jonathan Ogden and ferocious middle linebacker Ray Lewis. The 6-foot-9 and 340-pound Ogden was known for his enormous strength, quick feet, and keen understanding of the game. Lewis, who had played for the powerhouse University of Miami Hurricanes in college, was a fierce tackler who added a confident swagger to the defense.

The Ravens got off to a fine start in Baltimore, winning their home opener 19–14 over the Oakland Raiders in front of 64,000 fans in Memorial Stadium. Ogden and Lewis were key components in that victory and throughout the season. Lewis made a team-leading 95 tackles his rookie season, and Ogden provided wall-like protection for Testaverde, who used the time to throw for 4,177 yards—including a whopping 429 in a single game against the St. Louis Rams—and 33 touchdown passes. Many of Testaverde's passes ended up in the hands of fleet-footed wide receivers Michael Jackson and Derrick Alexander, who each put up more than 1,000 receiving yards on the season.

Despite the efforts of their veteran quarterback and dynamic rookies, the Ravens went a disappointing 4–12 in 1996. The club won half of its home games but lost all eight games on the road. "We took our share of lumps this year," said Coach Marchibroda. "But we had a lot of young players do a lot of growing up. We'll get better."

Vinny Testaverde played 21 seasons in the NFL (with 7 different teams), but he never experienced a finer statistical year than he did in 1996. **X**

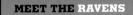

JONATHAN OGDEN

OFFENSIVE TACKLE
RAVENS SEASONS: 1996-2007
HEIGHT: 6-FOOT-9
WEIGHT: 340 POUNDS

Jonathan Ogden was a mountain of a man, even by NFL standards. Although his size and power were obvious, what made him unique were his nimble feet and intelligent approach to the game. Like most great offensive linemen, Ogden toiled in relative obscurity. Since the only time a spotlight shines on an offensive lineman during a game is when he commits a penalty or is beaten on a play, Ogden received little fanfare. Yet the Ravens recognized how special he was, rewarding him in 2000 with a $44-million contract, the largest in league history for an offensive lineman at the time. Opponents thought highly of Ogden as well. "You have to try to keep him off-balance, but he is so big and his arms are so big that it is hard to do," said New York Giants defensive end Cedric Jones. "I bet you could put him anywhere on the field and he would do all right." The future Hall-of-Famer always seemed to make the most of the opportunities given to him, catching two career passes ... for two total yards and two touchdowns.

Baltimore's biggest weakness its first season was a soft defense. In the 1997 NFL Draft, the team addressed that shortcoming by selecting fast linebackers Peter Boulware and Jamie Sharper. After the draft, the team also signed huge defensive tackle Tony "The Goose" Siragusa. Siragusa, whose barrel-shaped body looked ill-suited for professional football, became an instant fan favorite with his bulldozing playing style and colorful personality.

These newcomers helped the 1997 Ravens improve to 6–9–1. Boulware was particularly outstanding, making 11.5 quarterback sacks to earn the NFL's Defensive Rookie of the Year award. Lewis and Ogden, meanwhile, only got better, as the linebacker made an NFL-high 156 stops, while the tackle opened big holes for running backs Byron "Bam" Morris and Earnest Byner.

Before the start of the 1998 season, Baltimore added two new defensive backs, one a youngster and one a veteran. The team drafted quick rookie cornerback Duane Starks, then added experienced leadership to its core of young talent by signing defensive back Rod Woodson. A 7-time Pro-Bowler during his 10-year career with the Pittsburgh Steelers, Woodson was a crafty ballhawk who still had great speed.

X Peter Boulware led the nation in sacks during his final college season, and he continued to torment quarterbacks at the NFL level, averaging 10 sacks a year in his first 5 seasons.

X Located just south of Baltimore's pro baseball stadium, Oriole Park, PSINet Stadium (today called M&T Bank Stadium) rose 185 feet high.

Along with these new players, the 1998 Ravens had a new home. After playing their first two seasons at old Memorial Stadium, the team moved into the beautiful new Ravens Stadium at Camden Yards in downtown Baltimore (which was renamed PSINet Stadium in January 1999). "Playing at Memorial Stadium was great, but it still sort of belonged to the Colts," said receiver Michael Jackson. "This place is all ours."

The thrill of the new stadium did not improve the Ravens' fortunes, though. The defense was solid, and 5-foot-7 receiver Jermaine Lewis emerged as perhaps the league's most electrifying kick returner. But a suddenly sputtering offense

X Jermaine Lewis set a national high school record in the 200-meter dash before putting his speed to use for Baltimore as a kick return specialist.

THE MEN IN THE MIDDLE

Many football historians regard the 2000 Ravens as the best defensive team in NFL history. The statistics certainly support that conclusion, as that Ravens squad surrendered the meager averages of 10.3 points and 60.6 rushing yards per game—both league records. And even though the team's great linebackers received most of the accolades, the players most responsible for the success of that season and the 2001 campaign might have been massive defensive tackles Sam Adams and Tony Siragusa. Although slow, their bulk (nearly 350 pounds each) and power enabled Adams and Siragusa to devour running backs who ran up the middle, or else to draw double-team blocking, meaning that players such as Ray Lewis could make tackles while facing few blockers. "We won the Super Bowl in 2000," Ray Lewis later acknowledged, "because we had two guys in front of me that told me, 'You will not be touched.'" The Ravens' defense slipped a bit after Adams and "The Goose" left town in 2002, but in 2006, Baltimore tried to return to its winning formula by drafting another huge run-stuffer, defensive tackle Haloti Ngata.

caused the team to stumble to a 6–10 finish. Perhaps the biggest highlight of the year occurred late in the season when the Colts returned to town. The Ravens fell behind but surged back with 25 points in the second half to beat Indianapolis in a 38–31 shootout. Disappointed with the team's lack of progress, Baltimore fired Coach Marchibroda after the season.

The Ravens' point-scoring woes in 1998 led them to look for an offense-minded coach. After interviewing several prospects, Baltimore chose Minnesota Vikings offensive coordinator Brian Billick. During his seven years with the Vikings, Billick had put together one of the most fearsome offenses the NFL had ever seen. During the 1998 season, Minnesota had scored an NFL-record 556 points, with 38 of those points coming in a 38–28 victory over the Ravens. "We had identified Brian as one of the top young coaches in the game," said Art Modell. "But after that performance, we became convinced that he would be our top choice."

Billick examined the Ravens' roster and saw a lopsided team. The improving defense was already among the best in the league. With the great linebacking trio of Lewis, Boulware, and Sharper; a stout defensive line that included Siragusa and ends Rob Burnett and Michael McCrary; and speedy defensive backs such as Woodson, Starks, and cornerback

Chris McAllister, the Ravens could put a stranglehold on opposing offenses. But with the exception of Ogden, Baltimore's offense had just mediocre ability.

Billick loved coordinating offenses that featured high-powered passing attacks. In Baltimore, though, he realized he didn't have the type of talent needed to run an explosive offense through the air. Instead, he installed a low-risk, run-oriented offense, choosing to play conservatively with the ball and rely on his fierce defense to hold opponents down.

In 1999, the Ravens stumbled to a 3–6 start. But in the middle of the season, the team took flight, averaging 26

Although he made only one trip to the Pro Bowl in his career, end Rob Burnett was a valuable defender for a long time, spending six seasons in Cleveland and six more in Baltimore. **X**

Tony Siragusa's girth made him nearly immovable on the Ravens' defensive line, and his loud, colorful personality earned him television opportunities after his playing days. **X**

MEET THE RAVENS

RAY LEWIS

LINEBACKER
RAVENS SEASONS: 1996–PRESENT
HEIGHT: 6-FOOT-1
WEIGHT: 250 POUNDS

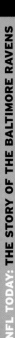

Dick Butkus. Lawrence Taylor. Ray Lewis. Such is the reputation of Ray Lewis that any discussion of the greatest linebackers in NFL history must include "Ray-Ray." Number 52 had it all: great instincts, good speed, and vicious hitting power. As Miami Dolphins general manager Randy Mueller said, "He wants to break someone in half each time he hits them." Lewis's ability was made evident by the slew of awards won during his career—two NFL Defensive Player of the Year awards (2000 and 2003), a Super Bowl Most Valuable Player (MVP) award, and nine Pro Bowl selections. But what truly elevated him into the realm of all-time greats was the passion and vocal leadership he brought onto the field. Fellow Ravens defenders played with an extra bit of energy for fear of letting Lewis down. Lewis's legacy was tarnished somewhat in February 2000, when he was charged with murder after two men were killed outside an Atlanta nightclub during a Super Bowl party. He was ultimately cleared of the most serious charges and came back to lead his team to victory in the Super Bowl a year later.

X Receiver Qadry "The Missile" Ismail (his more famous football-playing brother Raghib was nicknamed "The Rocket") averaged 16 yards a catch during the 1999 season.

points per game the rest of the year. Much of the offensive spark came from backup quarterback Tony Banks and receiver Qadry Ismail. Banks stepped in at midseason and tossed 17 touchdown passes, while Ismail—a speedster nicknamed "The Missile"—piled up more than 1,000 receiving yards. Behind these efforts and the NFL's second-ranked defense, Baltimore won five of its last seven games to finish 8–8. "We've built a little fire here," said Coach Billick. "It will be interesting to see how big it gets."

A SUPER DEFENSE

X

X Known more for a good work ethic than natural talent, quarterback Trent Dilfer spent only one season in Baltimore but made the most of it, helping the Ravens fly to the Super Bowl.

Hoping to add fuel to their fire, the Ravens used the fifth overall pick of the 2000 NFL Draft to select University of Tennessee running back Jamal Lewis, a big, powerful ballcarrier with the ability to wear down opposing defenses. The Ravens also added offensive firepower by signing veteran tight end Shannon Sharpe and quarterback Trent Dilfer. Sharpe, a longtime star with the Denver Broncos, gave the Ravens a sure-handed target, while Dilfer, a former starter with the Tampa Bay Buccaneers, was signed to serve as Banks's backup.

The Ravens soared to a 5–1 start in 2000. The fearsome defense led the way, not allowing a single point in three of those six games. But oddly, the Ravens offense, which had looked so promising at the end of the previous season, got worse in 2000. Banks's performance was marked by interceptions, fumbles, and inaccuracy as the Ravens went four straight games without scoring an offensive touchdown.

Looking for an offensive spark and fewer mistakes,

BRIAN BILLICK

COACH
RAVENS SEASONS: 1999-2007

Brian Billick was sometimes accused of being arrogant, a personality trait he did not deny. "If being arrogant is having self-confidence," he once said, "then I'm arrogant." That self-confidence—along with a willingness to adapt—helped Billick rise to the top of the NFL. When he was named the Ravens' head coach in 1999, Baltimore was going into its fourth season, having posted losing records its first three. Less than two years later, the Ravens were Super Bowl champions, and they returned to the grand stage of the NFL playoffs in two of the three seasons after that. Billick, who had spent time playing both linebacker and tight end in college, earned his coaching chance in Baltimore due to his offensive genius. But, surprisingly, he ended up building a team known for its ferocious, record-setting defense. His players in Baltimore appreciated his direct and assured leadership style. "More than any coach I played for, Brian treated the players with respect and got the most out of us," said star safety Rod Woodson. "He always got to the heart of things, no bull."

Billick inserted Dilfer as the starting quarterback in the season's second half. The decision paid off, as Dilfer led the Ravens to seven straight victories. Dilfer was a solid field general, and Jamal Lewis rumbled for 1,364 rushing yards, but it was the Baltimore defense that made headlines. Ray Lewis and his fellow defenders surrendered only 165 total points—an NFL record for a 16-game season. This phenomenal effort carried the Ravens to a 12–4 record and their first playoff berth. "We're no offensive juggernaut," said Sharpe. "But we don't have to be. If we score 17 points, Ray and the 'D' will make it stick."

In the playoffs, the Ravens proved Sharpe correct, advancing to Super Bowl XXXV by beating the Denver Broncos, Tennessee Titans, and Oakland Raiders while allowing only 16 total points. In the Super Bowl, Baltimore faced a New York Giants team that had thrashed Minnesota 41–0 in its previous playoff game. But the Ravens could not be stopped. Dilfer hit receiver Brandon Stokley with a touchdown pass in the first quarter to open the scoring, Jermaine Lewis returned a kickoff 84 yards for another score in the third quarter, and the Ravens defense made four interceptions as Baltimore rolled to a 34–7 victory. Only a kick return for a touchdown kept the Giants from being shut

out. Two days later, more than 200,000 people turned out on a cold and rainy day in Baltimore to celebrate the victory with a parade. Art Modell, who finally had his championship after 40 years as an NFL owner, was overcome with emotion. "This," he said, "is the thrill of my life."

The Ravens shuffled their offensive lineup the next season, drafting talented tight end Todd Heap and making a change at quarterback, releasing Dilfer and signing former Kansas City Chiefs quarterback Elvis Grbac, who was considered a more polished passer. The Ravens were dealt a serious blow, however, when Jamal Lewis suffered a season-ending knee injury during training camp.

Despite the loss of their top running back, the Ravens put together a strong 10–6 season, beating the Vikings in the final game of the year to qualify for the playoffs. Hopes of a Super Bowl repeat ran high after Baltimore squashed the Miami Dolphins 20–3 in a first-round showdown. The win was a historic one, as it made the Ravens the first NFL team ever to win its first five playoff games. There would be no sixth straight win, though. The Ravens lost the next week, 27–10, to the rival Steelers.

THIRTY-SIX SUPER SECONDS

Super Bowl XXXV, after the 2000 season, was a defensive showcase, as Baltimore gave up just 152 yards of offense and crushed the New York Giants 34–7. But that championship game is also remembered for 36 seconds that have been called the most exciting in Super Bowl history. The drama started late in the third quarter, when Ravens cornerback Duane Starks intercepted a pass by Giants quarterback Kerry Collins and returned it 49 yards for a touchdown. On the ensuing kickoff, Giants kick returner Ron Dixon eluded the Ravens' coverage team and took the ball the length of the field for New York's only score of the game. Then the Ravens returned the favor. Small and shifty kick returner Jermaine Lewis (pictured) fielded the kickoff and wove his way over 84 yards of turf for a touchdown of his own. In three plays, 21 total points were put on the scoreboard—the fastest scoring flurry in Super Bowl history. "When we ran back our kick," said Baltimore coach Brian Billick, "it fueled us. And you could see the air go out of [the Giants]."

STARS AND
STRUGGLES

After the 2001 season, Baltimore let Sharpe and Woodson leave town, choosing to give Heap and rookie safety Ed Reed starting roles. Baltimore hoped the youth movement would energize the team, but unfortunately, the Ravens' bad luck with injuries continued as Ray Lewis suffered a separated shoulder that sidelined him for most of 2002. The Ravens' quarterback situation also took an unexpected turn when Grbac retired before the season, leaving veteran Jeff Blake and youngster Chris Redman to run the offense. Amid such turbulence, the 2002 Ravens faded to 7–9.

In the 2003 NFL Draft, the Ravens reinforced their lineup by selecting pass-rushing linebacker Terrell Suggs and quarterback Kyle Boller. Suggs had set a national collegiate record with 24 quarterback sacks during his final season at Arizona State University, while Boller impressed team coaches in training camp with his powerful throwing arm and earned the starting job as a rookie.

Baltimore's quarterback play remained shaky in 2003 as Boller was injured and replaced by Anthony Wright. The good news, though, was that the rest of the team began to resemble its old Super Bowl form. Jamal Lewis had the season of a lifetime, rushing for an incredible 2,066 yards—the second-highest total in NFL history. Ray Lewis was healthy

JAMAL LEWIS

RUNNING BACK
RAVENS SEASONS: 2000-06
HEIGHT: 5-FOOT-11
WEIGHT: 245 POUNDS

Jamal Lewis was a freakish running back. At a stocky, bull-necked 245 pounds, he had the ability to blast his way through defenders like a battering ram. Yet he was also amazingly light on his feet, able to dance around linebackers and then outrun defensive backs. During his seven seasons in a Ravens uniform, Lewis experienced the highest of highs and the lowest of lows. He helped Baltimore win the Super Bowl as a rookie in 2000, then tore a knee ligament in training camp the next year and missed the entire 2001 season. Back to form by 2003, he galloped into NFL history with an incredible 2,066-yard rushing effort (including one game with 295 rushing yards, which was then a league record). A year later, Lewis made headlines of the wrong kind, as he was charged with drug trafficking and sentenced to four months in prison—a term he served before the start of the 2005 season. The Ravens, looking to try a new offensive approach, let Lewis leave town after the 2006 season. He then signed with the rival Cleveland Browns, who had re-entered the league in 1999.

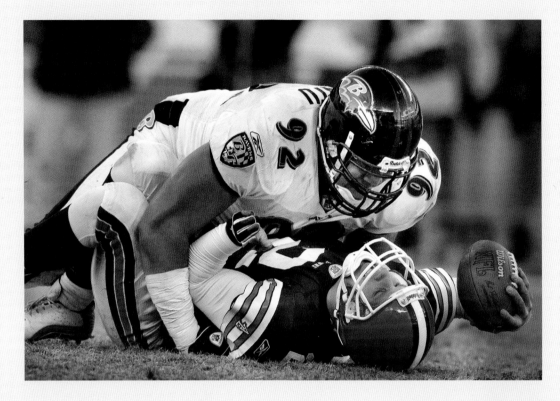

again and back to his dominant ways, winning his second NFL

Defensive Player of the Year award. Suggs racked up 12 sacks

to win the Defensive Rookie of the Year award, and linebacker

Adalius Thomas emerged as a star with his aggressive special-

teams tackling. These efforts helped the Ravens win their

first AFC North Division championship (the NFL's divisions had

been realigned in 2002) with a 10–6 record, but the season

ended bitterly with a 20–17 loss to the Titans in the playoffs.

The 2004 season kicked off with a new team owner in

Baltimore. Art Modell, who was then 78 years old, had sold

majority ownership of the team to Baltimore businessman

X Although he
went undrafted out
of college, 350-pound
tackle Ma'ake
Kemoeatu made his
impact felt as part of
the Ravens' defense
from 2002 to 2005.

Steve Bisciotti in April 2004. Unfortunately, after paying the $600-million asking price, Bisciotti watched an unfortunate trend unfold in Baltimore. While the defense—led by the passionate play of Ray Lewis, Reed, Thomas, and veteran cornerback Deion Sanders—remained one of the NFL's scariest, the Ravens' offense bordered on inept. Jamal Lewis managed just 1,006 yards on the year, and Travis Taylor led all Ravens receivers with a meager 421 yards. Injuries compounded Baltimore's troubles, and the Ravens finished the year 9–7 and out of the playoffs. The finish left the players disappointed. "It's disheartening to think that we're going to be one of those teams that's watching everyone else play in January," Ravens defensive end Marques Douglas said. "We want to be one of those elite teams, and this year, we're not."

The woes of 2004—a feeble offensive attack and injuries to key players—repeated themselves in 2005. Neither Wright nor Boller could get the offense in gear, and Jamal Lewis struggled after an off-season that included knee surgery and a four-month prison sentence on drug charges. The Ravens went 0–8 on the road and mustered just a 6–10 record overall.

A RUSH OF RECORDS

After the Ravens' dominant run to the Super Bowl in 2000, the 2001 season—despite its 10–6 record and playoff victory—was a letdown. But even though the Ravens' faithful weren't able to cheer for their heroes on Super Bowl Sunday again, they did get to watch several Baltimore stars set new NFL records that season. On November 18, Shannon Sharpe (pictured), the longtime Denver Broncos star known for his bulging biceps and talkative nature, set a new league receiving record for tight ends when he snagged the 663rd catch of his career. Not to be outdone, cornerback Rod Woodson—who had already played a Hall of Fame-caliber career in Pittsburgh before signing with Baltimore—made NFL history two weeks later by scoring the 10th interception-return touchdown of his career. In that same game against the Colts, longtime Browns and Ravens kicker Matt Stover set an NFL record by booting a field goal in his 38th straight game. While Sharpe and Woodson moved on to other teams after that season, Stover remained in Baltimore, kicking in his 18th NFL season by 2008.

McNAIR, McGAHEE, AND THE ROAD AHEAD

X--------------

Although 2005 ended with Baltimore's worst record in seven years, there were signs that a turnaround was coming. Late in the season, the Ravens had beaten their rivals, the defending Super Bowl champion Steelers, 16–13, and obliterated the Green Bay Packers 48–3. After the season, the team made a move to improve its long-struggling quarterback play, signing veteran passer Steve McNair from the Titans. Although McNair was on the downside of his career, he was a former league MVP known for his toughness. Billick believed that with McNair throwing the ball to such up-and-coming receivers as Mark Clayton, the Ravens' offense might at last come close to matching the strength of its defense. McNair agreed. "I think this is a place we can win Super Bowls," he said. "That is the missing piece out of my career."

McNair's calm leadership and willingness to play through pain seemed to inspire his teammates in 2006. The Ravens started the season with a four-game winning streak and ended it with four straight wins for a 13–3 record and another AFC North title. The defense, featuring such newcomers as big rookie tackle Haloti Ngata and veteran end Trevor Pryce, was resilient in the playoffs against the high-powered Indianapolis Colts, surrendering five field goals but no touchdowns. Unfortunately, McNair threw two

X Hoping to develop a passing game as strong as their rushing attack, the Ravens selected scrappy wide receiver Mark Clayton with the 22nd pick of the 2005 NFL Draft.

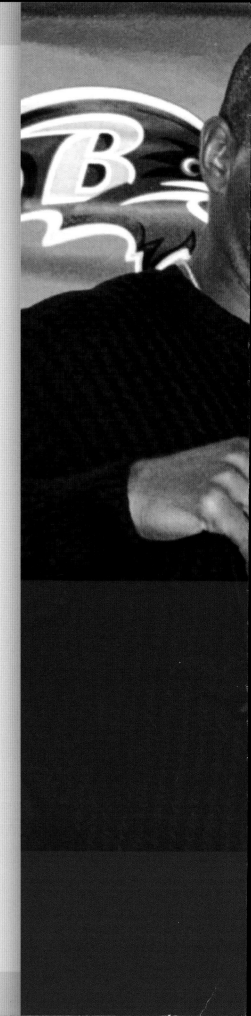

interceptions, Todd Heap lost a critical fumble, and Baltimore fell by a score of 15–6.

The Ravens let Jamal Lewis leave town after the season and replaced him with former Buffalo Bills halfback Willis McGahee. A versatile runner just entering the prime of his career, the 26-year-old McGahee had averaged 1,122 yards a year in his three seasons in Buffalo, and he galloped for 1,207 in a Ravens jersey in 2007. Unfortunately, he was one of few bright spots in the most disappointing season in team history. The Ravens started out 4–2 but then collapsed, losing nine games in a row. The most embarrassing defeat came at the hands of the Miami Dolphins, who were 0–13 before beating the Ravens 22–16 late in the season. McNair struggled before he was benched late in the season and replaced by Kyle Boller, and the once-impenetrable defense surrendered at least 27 points in 8 games. The dramatic drop-off prompted team owner Steve Bisciotti to fire Coach Billick the day after the season ended.

Hired as Billick's replacement was John Harbaugh, who had spent the previous 10 seasons as an assistant coach with the Philadelphia Eagles. Harbaugh inherited a team that he believed could quickly climb back among the AFC's elite—and he was right. Although Ray Lewis was entering the twilight of

STAPLES

OZZIE'S WIZARDRY

As a star tight end for the Cleveland Browns in the 1980s, Ozzie Newsome (pictured, left) set an NFL record with 662 pass receptions (a mark later broken by Ravens tight end Shannon Sharpe) and became known as the "Wizard of Oz." But Newsome's nickname seemed most appropriate after his playing days were over, when he became the "man behind the curtain" for the Ravens. As Baltimore's vice president of player personnel (starting in 1996) and then as its general manager (starting in 2002), Newsome was the brain behind the Ravens' NFL Draft selections and free-agent signings, and he was widely regarded as a genius at recognizing and obtaining talent. He was credited with building the roster that won Super Bowl XXXV, and over the course of a decade, he put such stars as Ray Lewis, Jonathan Ogden, Jamal Lewis, Todd Heap, and Ed Reed in Ravens purple. In 2005, *Sports Illustrated* writer Don Banks identified Newsome as the league's sharpest personnel mind, writing that "the Ravens are the NFL's gold standard on draft day, consistently making choices that stand the test of time."

ON THE SIDELINES

RING OF RAVENS

Most players in the NFL do not have long careers—only about four years on average. But the truly great ones play on forever in the minds of their fans. The Baltimore Ravens have a special fraternity to commemorate their greats: the Ring of Honor. This elite club welcomes only those members of the Ravens family who have demonstrated seven special traits: character, gratitude, vision, passion, courage, a competitive spirit, and humility. The first man to enter the Ring was dependable running back Earnest Byner, who was inducted in 2001. Since that time, team owner Art Modell, defensive end Michael McCrary, and linebacker Peter Boulware have joined the Ring as well. Their names—along with those of quarterback Johnny Unitas and the seven other Baltimore Colts legends enshrined in the Pro Football Hall of Fame—are displayed on big signs along the interior façade that encircles Baltimore's M&T Bank Stadium (formerly PSINet Stadium). Boulware, the most recent inductee (in 2006), was thrilled by the honor. "There's so much great history in this city," he said, "and to be a part of that is awesome."

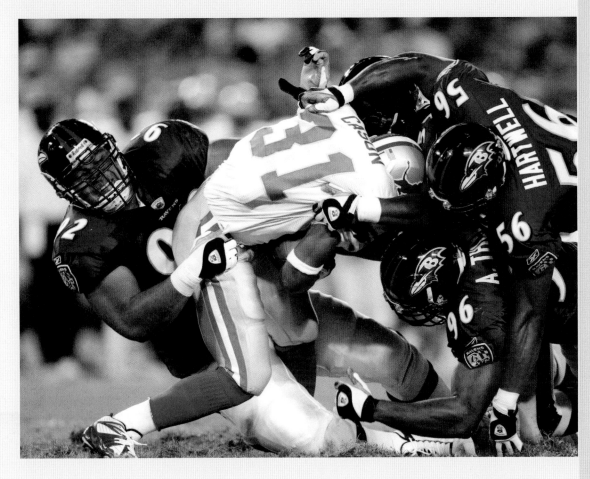

his career, his inspirational leadership and the outstanding play of Reed, Suggs, and linebacker Bart Scott made Baltimore an AFC North beast again in 2008. Although the offense was still not overpowering, the Ravens began scoring more points late in the season as rookie quarterback Joe Flacco showed veteran-like poise.

After Baltimore's 11–5 record secured a Wild Card spot in the playoffs, the Ravens made a run at another Super Bowl. First they squashed the Dolphins, 27–9, then they knocked out the top-seeded Titans, 13–10. But there would be no third

X An almost impenetrable defense has been the Ravens' trademark for nearly a decade; Baltimore ranked second in the NFL against the run in both 2006 and 2007.

X In 2007, new Ravens halfback Willis McGahee bulled through opposing defenses en route to the third 1,000-yard season of his career and first Pro Bowl.

ED REED

SAFETY
RAVENS SEASONS: 2002-PRESENT
HEIGHT: 5-FOOT-11
WEIGHT: 200 POUNDS

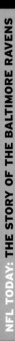

NFL TODAY: THE STORY OF THE BALTIMORE RAVENS

Like Ray Lewis, Ed Reed played college football at the University of Miami. And although he was smaller and quieter than Lewis, he played with the same swagger and toughness. After being selected with the 24th overall pick in the 2002 NFL Draft, Reed started every game his rookie season. Naturally fast and fearless, he was also an intelligent player who sought a mental edge by studying game film to learn his opponents' tendencies. The star safety could do it all. In 2002, he blocked the first two punts in Ravens history, returning one for a touchdown. In 2004, he picked off an NFL-high 9 passes and returned one of them 106 yards for a touchdown— the longest scoring play in NFL history at the time. Such efforts cemented his status as, arguably, the game's best safety and earned him the 2004 NFL Defensive Player of the Year award. Still, Reed insisted he could get better. "I have a lot more to learn," he said. "Just like any other thing in life, you want to continue being a student at whatever it is you do."

straight road victory. Facing the Steelers in a hard-hitting AFC Championship Game, Flacco tossed three interceptions, and Baltimore lost 23–14. Still, Coach Harbaugh loved his players' effort. "I couldn't be more proud to stand with them in victory and, today, in defeat," he said.

The Baltimore Ravens have packed a lot of excitement into a history that spans barely a decade. Boasting one Super Bowl victory, perhaps the greatest defense in NFL history, and a collection of sure-fire Hall-of-Famers that includes Ray Lewis and Jonathan Ogden, the team in the purple uniforms has resurrected Baltimore's football tradition in a big way—and hopes to roost atop the NFL again very soon.

Thanks in large part to the always intimidating Ravens "D," John Harbaugh won his first two games—and first two playoff games—as an NFL head coach in 2008. **X**

INDEX